Painting Porcelain in the Meissen Style

Painting Porcelain in the Meissen Style

Uwe Geissler

Schiffer Publishing Ltd
4880 Lower Valley Road, Atglen, PA 19310 USA

Hearty thanks for their help and support in completing this book to Manuela, Katharina and Daddy Helmut

Library of Congress Cataloging-in-Publication Data:

Geissler, Uwe.
[Porzellan bemalen auf Meissner Art. English]
Painting porcelain the Meissen way/Uwe Geissler; [translated by Edward Force].
p. cm.
Published simultaneously in Germany.
Includes bibliographical references.
ISBN: 978-0-7643-0280-0 (paper)
1. China painting—Technique. 2. Meissen porcelain—Themes, motives. I. Title.
NK4605.G4313 1997
738.1'5—dc21 97-19519
CIP

Originally published as *Porzellan bemalen auf Meißner Art: Vorlagen für Fortgeschrittene*
By Georg D.W. Callwey GmbH & Co., Munich

Translated by Dr. Edward Force,
Central Connecticut State University

ISBN: 978-0-7643-0280-0
Printed in China

Frontispiece:
A typical scene from the studio of a Meissen porcelain painter.

Published by Schiffer Publishing Ltd.
4880 Lower Valley Road
Atglen, PA 19310
Phone: (610) 593-1777; Fax: (610) 593-2002
E-mail: Info@schifferbooks.com

In Europe, Schiffer books are distributed by
Bushwood Books
6 Marksbury Ave.
Kew Gardens
Surrey TW9 4JF England
Phone: 44 (0) 20 8392 8585; Fax: 44 (0) 20 8392 9876
E-mail: info@bushwoodbooks.co.uk
Website: www.bushwoodbooks.co.uk

Contents

Foreword

When I began the work of writing the book "Porcelain Painting" in 1986, I was soon made aware of how much effort I probably would have to spend to write a book that could perhaps lose its timeliness all too soon to a new "hobby wave".

Today I am still sitting at the easel, and at the typewriter again, and finding the time to complete the information that I compiled then. I am happy to find that a great many amateur painters have remained loyal to this metier and look forward to new patterns and directions for the advanced painter. There are even some among them who—similarly to the porcelain crafters—"have turpentine in their blood." Through many years of practice, and with much diligence, they have, completely on their own, developed a painting style that is worthy of being seen internationally.

Thanks to the new political situation in Germany, which finally makes it possible to exchange experience and knowledge, my friends in Meissen no longer remain anonymous, nameless numbers. Since the opening of the border, there is active contact between the show painters and the instructors, which spreads the great tradition of porcelain painting further. Since Meissen represents this devotion to tradition in an outstanding manner, one may now hope that every porcelain devotee in all of Europe will gain new inspirations for this handicraft, which has come to be a rarity.

Unfortunately, this great interest also calls out self-styled artists who never painted a stroke at Meissen and yet want to teach the "original Meissen" flower painting. Nor do they avoid publication. This naturally includes the danger of losing quality in the traditional motifs and does not do the hobby painter any good. Only a single, very special style of painting can be called the Meissen manner. Every old veteran Meissen painter rightfully says, "You have only learned it right after ten years. Then you begin to develop your own personal style!"

All of this was reason enough for me to reveal the complete palette of Meissen flowers and direct attention to a high-quality painting style. To the trained professional painter it is not sufficient for a rose to look "similar" to the Meissen manner. Plenty of porcelain producers achieve such results. Thankfully, many porcelain fans are no longer satisfied with painting that really belongs in a souvenir shop. In a time when even large-scale manufacturers have to accept criticism when apprentices' work is offered at high prices, we hope increasing quality, and not just trade marks, will become the critical factor in demand. My efforts also apply to this goal.

With the book at hand, I would particularly like to address the painter who has several years of experience. Thematically, there will thus be no explanations for beginners. The subjects treated in addition to flower painting were chosen partly according to readers' wishes and thus offer a deliberate enrichment of the decoration variations already treated. The wishes of many students of painting to learn more about underglaze painting were also considered. In particular, the painting of wild fruits and hunting scenes, which belong to naturalistic decoration and are very well handled in painting courses, were included, even though they are used rarely on manufactured goods. Surely this fact increases the charm of such motifs. I have taken most of the examples from my patterns, which I prepared in Meissen from 1973 to 1982, and that still serve as models to the painters there today. They are passed on from class to class, from generation to generation, and appear to us again and again in slightly modified form when we look at the various products.

There are genuine "classics" of certain bouquets which, newly interpreted by different flowers or color nuances, turn up again and again. But in all the other sections of Meissen decoration there are also these classic models. For many years, Meissen fans have been familiar with the Wendler rose, the Ming dragon by Matthes, copperplates by Meiner, Old Fruits and Flowers by Knobloch, birds by Kegel, fruits by Bretschneider, as well as the "prickly" brooch paintings of Pelke. Paintings by these personalities have served, and still serve, many porcelain painters in Meissen as patterns and thus find worldwide acclaim. If you value learning the original Meissen manner, try, when possible, to obtain models of genuine Meissen porcelain painting. Take photos of pieces at exhibitions, buy the Meissen good-wish cards, which were designed by manufacturers.

I. Naturalistically painted Alpine flowers, such as the Edelweiss shown here, are not included in the Meissen flower assortment, but are very popular among nature lovers. This is a study by the author.

In all our efforts to know the Meissen original as well as possible, we must take note of certain decorations that are copyrighted and cannot be painted in the original form. This primarily concerns patterns in which crossed swords are seen, as well as the onion pattern or various Indian motifs. The swords clearly symbolize their origin in Meissen; they are absolutely taboo for the hobby painter and cannot be imitated on unmarked whiteware. This would be an obvious attempt to falsify, and would justly be opposed most severely by the manufacturers if such a piece should turn up in the trade or at an art auction. If you want to have a go at one of the unique designs made by the artists of the Meissen development department, found in the most varied form on wall plates and the like, then it is best to mark your work as "painted after . . ." and add your initials as your own signature. In the choice of my drawings and photographic examples, I have chosen only the best designs, in order to challenge the already proficient painter's ability more than ever before. For him this should be a stimulus to take another step on the road to perfection, which has no end.

Painting on the Glaze

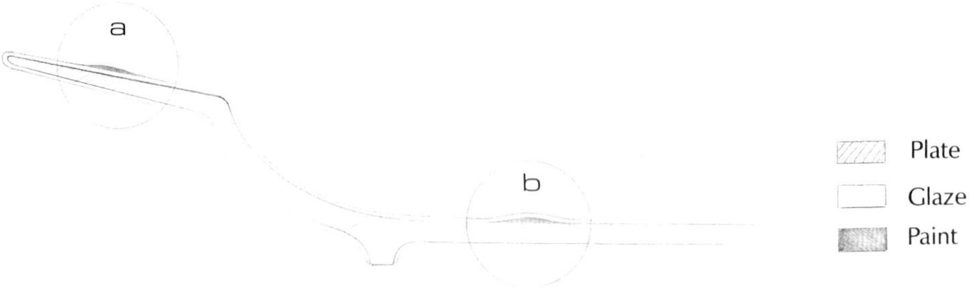

II. Cross-section of a plate, showing the positions of the over-glaze paint (a) and underglaze paint (b) on the plate.

Concept

Since even students of painting who have practiced for several years still ask, I should like to explain briefly the essential difference between on- and underglaze painting once again.

Out of a malleable mass of porcelain, the subsequent porcelain objects are made by casting, turning or free forming. When these objects are dried well (either in the plaster form or in air), they are subjected to a first burning at 750 to 1050 degrees Celsius. Now they are firm enough to be treated further, but still unglazed. In this condition, the pieces can be decorated with underglaze paint. The pattern is applied and dried well. Since the piece is still very porous and thus absorbent, one has to work quickly in order to form clear contours and thin lines.

Only then is the piece given a glaze. One must imagine it as a thin, milky liquid coating, which, at first, fully covers the decoration. As a rule, glazing is done by dipping in the glaze or airbrushing with a spray gun. It appears as a white coating which, only in the ensuing burning, becomes transparent, and now it forms a protective coat of glass over the painting—thoroughly sealing the object.

If this sealing is applied directly after the first burning, resulting in thoroughly hardened white porcelain, the pieces are ready for over-glaze painting.

Cross-section of a Plate

In Illustration II we see a cross-section drawing showing the location of the painting below and above the glaze. The work processes thus run as follows:

Underglaze: raw piece—decoration—glazing;
Over-glaze: raw piece—glazing—decoration.

Advantages and Disadvantages

Over-glaze painting amounts to the largest percentage of decoration on porcelain today. For the stencil patterns used by many porcelain makers today too, over-glaze painting dominates, even though underglaze decoration is more durable because the glaze protects it. This brings us to the only real disadvantage of over-glaze painting, namely its vulnerability to mechanical or chemical action. A fine hand-painting suffers from daily contact with knives, hard scrubbing brushes frequently used at hotels, rough cleansing agents, or dishwashers. Even stacking dishes one on top of another brings the danger of scratching the decoration. To be sure, the possessor of hand-painted dishes is usually happy to spend the time to wash them by hand. And only in rare cases are such dishes in daily use.

Nevertheless, the relatively easy removability of over-glaze painting has one advantage for us painters: after burning, we can "remove" any bad spots and correct them. This is, of course, a work process that requires much fingertip feeling and should be practiced as little as possible—but for the sake of completeness, I would like to mention it briefly here.

For the painter of fruit motifs, for example, where many colors, as is well known, become mixed when applied wet on wet, it can happen that during burning, spots in the painting react with each other too "strongly" and simply get cooked up or away. Just as easily, colors can be created that absolutely do not belong in the picture.

Cutting, Etching and Rubbing

With over-glaze paints, as already mentioned, one has the opportunity to improve without having to remove the entire picture. The spot in question is polished with a very fine grindstone under running water, or with an appropriate abrasive fluid (available in the trade) until the color either has been sufficiently lightened or has disappeared altogether. In this work process, small grinding or boring machines, such as glass engravers use, are usually used. They have a flexible shaft with which one can even reach "hidden" areas (such as on figures). But I have also heard from painters who have asked their dentist to remove a small spot of color that was burned in by mistake. If you want to try it yourself, please be sure to choose a very small grinder and begin by making a test operation on an old piece. In this type of paint removal, the glaze is usually not harmed when the work is done properly, and only seldom is it cut at all, and that can be covered with the new decoration. In the factories this process is used now and then on apprentices' work that is not completely successful but that need not be discarded because of one or two painting errors on the piece. After improving the spots in question, the piece can still be sold as a second. A layman will not notice such spots at all.

Even though there are far fewer iron flecks or bubbles to be seen in today's porcelain than there were twenty or more years ago, no manufacturer can turn out an unending stream of absolutely faultless porcelain. Thus it is totally a matter of the over-glaze painting that allows many seconds to be sold as first-class work.

Another method is the etching away of paint particles with acids. Primarily liquid acids are used for this, but I would rather not recommend them to the hobbyist. These liquids are very dangerous and should really be used only with strict safety measures. A little slip in applying it can have disastrous results—and that is really not worth the ruin of a porcelain motif. But perhaps there is a laboratory in your area that could do this work for you; thus I recommend this possibility. Here the firmly burned-in paint can be loosened and removed with the help of the acid. A very quick process is called for, of course, since the acid will also attack the glaze in time and can sometimes even expose the porcelain itself. In such situations, no brightly glowing paint can be applied any more. So in any case it is advantageous to leave this work process to a professional.

Burned-in paint can also be removed with glass-etching acid. It is very aggressive and dulls the piece after only a short time. I myself often use it on fantasy motifs, in which certain spots are supposed to have a matte look. The white porcelain is first etched to remove its gloss, and only then is it painted.

For the removal of mistakes in gold, the trade offers a solution that is very easy to use and can also be used easily by the layman: the gold eraser. This is a rod with a tip resembling hard rubber, available in various strengths. It easily removes all kinds of gold paint, as well as the thinnest bits of porcelain paint. In erasing, varying pressure should be used when rubbing the area in question. This covers the subject of "backward painting," as we porcelain painters say.

The preceding lines, though, should not let one forget that over-glaze painting is inherently very durable and is firmly united with the glaze, depending on the burning temperature. In the case of handpainted porcelain, we are usually dealing with decorative objects which are seldom subjected to a lot of mechanical abrasion.

Decoration Variations

The history of over-glaze painting is as old and varied as porcelain itself. I do not want to discuss it in depth, as there are plenty of reference works that cover the history and techniques of "white gold." Here we are concerned with the decorations and their formation. We could exaggerate slightly and say that in over-glaze technique, every painting style, every nuance of color is possible, as well as every motif taken from nature and any other subject can be painted. When you look at the thousands of pieces in all the museums, books or private collections, you see everything represented. Today one can define two basic painting trends for this technique, and they have existed in these forms for a long time:

Artistic decorations: Flower painting in a certain manner. Naturalistic painting with the subgroups of flowers, fruits, birds, landscapes, portraits, hunting scenes, and modern free compositions.

Graphic decorations: Indian painting in all its varieties and spectrum of colors, but also copperplates, monogram and script painting, plus most gold decorations, coats of arms, geometric designs and the like.

These two main groups are also "apportioned" to the drawing students in their first year at Meissen. It is tremendously important for their further training to know whether they are suited to painting or graphics and steered in the right direction. A drawing artist, who can create clear lines and delicate sketches easily and freely, would usually have a hard time painting a light, airy poppy with broad brush strokes. But this does not mean that one cannot learn both.

In the following chapters, I shall deal particularly with the decorations that were only handled briefly in the first two volumes on porcelain painting. I proceed from the premise that preparing the paints is already done and that the other preparations of brushes, dishes, oil and other utensils are familiar.

Let us now begin with the flower in the Meissen style. There are 36 so-called basic flowers, each of which will be presented in a three-part, step-by-step process.

III. The light, gentle touch used in Meissen around 1920. Wide strokes, gentle coloring and a "fresh" composition give this bouquet a very decorative note.

1-36. The 36 traditional Meissen flowers (see pages 9-11).

Meissen Flower Painting

The 36 Most Often Used Flower Motifs

1. Crocus
2. Plumed Poppy
3. Morning Glory
4. Iris
5. Daisy
6. Carnation
7. Fuchsia
8. Tulip
9. Columbine
10. Ranunculus
11. Garden Poppy
12. Double Rose
13. Nasturtium
14. Corn Poppy
15. Chinese Aster
16. Cornflower
17. Narcissus
18. Poppy Anemone
19. Dog-rose
20. Marigold
21. Sweet-pea
22. Hepatica
23. Pheasant's Eye
24. English Daisy
25. Larkspur
26. Marsh Marigold
27. Bleeding Heart
28. Violet
29. Hyacinth
30. Wallflower
31. Johnny Jump-Up
32. New York Aster
33. Primrose
34. Buttercup
35. Honeysuckle
36. Forget-Me-Not

All of these flowers are usable as the main flower in a motif—as well as scattered (except the fuchsia). Numbers 2 to 21 and 35 can also be used as secondary flowers. Numbers 3, 12, 13, 15, 17 to 19 and 21 to 34 can be used in garlands, and numbers 21, 24, 25, 29 and 36 in completing motifs.

1. Crocus, page 12

2. Plumed Poppy, page 12

3. Morning Glory, page 13

4. Iris, page 14

5. Ox-eye Daisy, page 15

6. Carnation, page 15

7. Fuchsia, page 16

8. Tulip, page 16

9. Columbine, page 17

10. Ranunculus, page 18

11. Poppy, page 19

12. Double Rose, page 20

13. Nasturtium, page 21

14. Corn Poppy, page 22

15. Chinese Aster, page 23

16. Cornflower, page 24

17. Narcissus, page 24

18. Poppy Anemone, page 25

19. Dog-rose, page 26

20. Marigold, page 26

21. Sweet Pea, page 27

22. Hepatica, page 28

23. Pheasant's Eye, page 28

24. English Daisy, page 29

25. Delphinium, page 30

26. Marsh Marigold, page 30

27. Bleeding Heart, page 31

28. Violet, page 32

29. Hyacinth, page 33

30. Wallflower, page 34

31. Johnny Jump-Up, page 35

32. New York Aster, page 35

33. Primrose, page 36

34. Buttercup, page 37

35. Honeysuckle, page 38

36. Forget-Me-Not, page 39

1. Crocus (Crocus vernus)

2. Plumed Poppy (Papaver)

3. Morning Glory (Ipomoea)

4. Iris (Iris versicolor)

5. Ox-eye Daisy (Chrysanthemum leucanthemum)

6. Carnation (Dianthus caryophyllus)

7. Fuchsia (Fuchsia coccinea)

8. Tulip (Tulipa)

9. Columbine (Aquilegia caerulea)

10. Ranunculus (Ranunculus asiaticus)

11. Poppy (Papaver)

12. Double Rose (Rosa)

13. Nasturtium (Tropaeolum majus)

14. Corn Poppy (Papaver rhoeas)

15. Chinese Aster (Aster chinensis)

16. Cornflower (Centaurea cyanus)

17. Narcissus (Narcissus pseudonarcissus)

18. Poppy Anemone (Anemone coronaria)

19. Dog-Rose (Rosa canina)

20. Marigold (Tagetes erecta)

21. Sweet Pea (Lathyrus odoratus)

22. Hepatiça (Hepatica)

23. Pheasant's Eye (Adonis aestivalis)

24. English Daisy (Bellis perennis)

25. Delphinium (Delphinium ajacis)

26. Marsh Marigold (Caltha palustris)

27. Bleeding Heart (Dicentra spectabilis)

28. Violet (Viola odorata)

29. Hyacinth (Hyacinthus orientalis)

30. Wallflower (Cheiranthus cheiri)

31. Johnny Jump-up (Viola tricolor)

32. New York Aster (Aster novi-belgii)

33. Primrose (Primula pubescens)

34. Buttercup (Ranunculus acris)

35. Honeysuckle (Lonicera caprifolium)

36. Forget-Me-Not (Myosotis arvensis)

37. Examples of old flower studies from Meissen. The paintings are not always "idealized," but show the flowers very naturalistically, with stiff stems, hanging heads, and in earthy colors: Dog-rose, poppy and narcissus.

38. "Heralds of spring," flower paintings in Meissen style, naturalistically portrayed from the painter's nature studies: marsh marigold, violet, morning glory, forget-me-not.

39, 40. Various painting subjects for direct transfer with a stencil.

39. Bouquet, narcissus, clover, wallflower and scattered flowers.

40. Double rose, cornflower, bouquet and sweet peas.

Combining Basic Flowers in Decorative Garlands

With the types of flowers shown, small or more luxurious flower arrangements can be created, as the customer wishes.

The basic differentiations are:

Variation 1 (#1-38): One of the previously shown flowers

Variation 2 (#41): One main flower with another added

Variation 3 (#42): One main flower with another attached and a third added

Variation 4 (#45): One main flower with second flower, attached flower and added flower

Bouquet (#44): More than five different flowers or petal colors.

All of these combinations can be painted in one color or more. The arrangement on the object in question is generally based on set patterns that have been created over the centuries. The exact placement can be studied best by looking at the originals. Note: The flowers become smaller in the decoration in the following order: Main flower—second flower—attached flower—added flower!

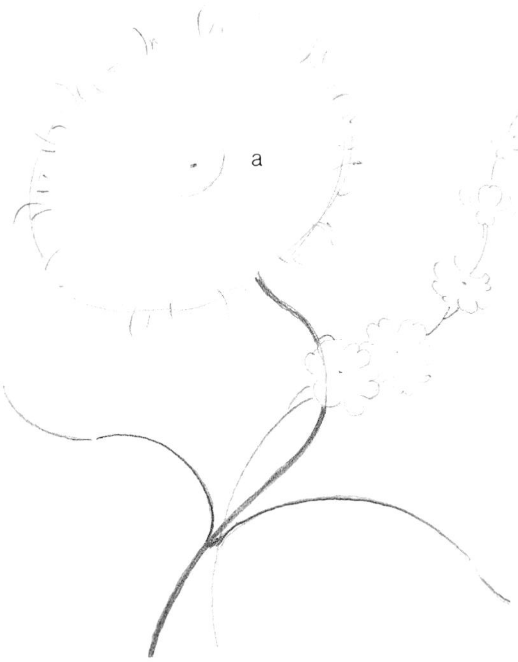

41-43. Various flower motifs, painted oval standing, and their arrangement on the string cross on the plate.

41. Example 1: main flower (a) and crossing (b).

42. Example 2: main flower (a), binding flower (b) and crossing (c).

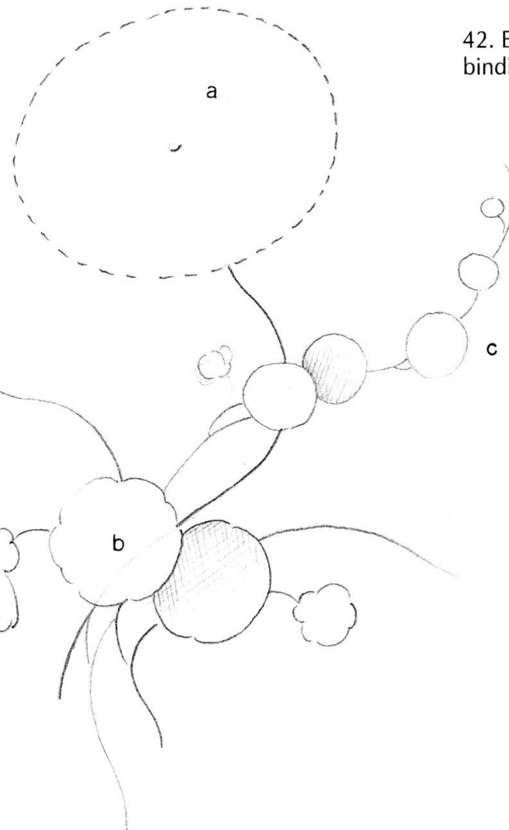

43. Example 3: arrangement in the string cross.

44. Classic Meissen bouquet with double rose, dog-roses, blue morning glories, sword lilies and scattered flowers.

45. Examples of composition of bouquets on plate flanges. The flowers can be chosen as you wish, so that various bouquets can be composed of the same basic pattern: main flower (a), second flower (b), binding flower (c), crossing (d).

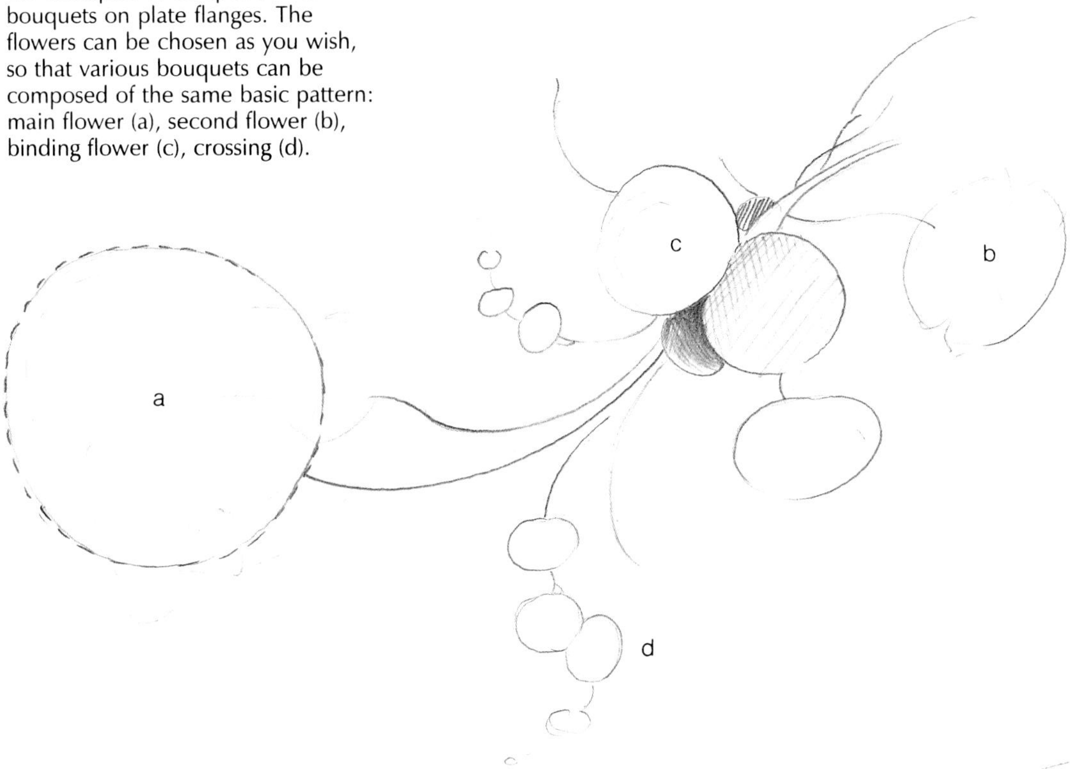

Ranunculus

Anemone

Pheasant's Eye

46. The leaf shapes of the various types of flowers should also be included in one's own color studies.

Plumed Poppy

Columbine

Aster

Marigold

Bleeding Heart

Marsh Marigold

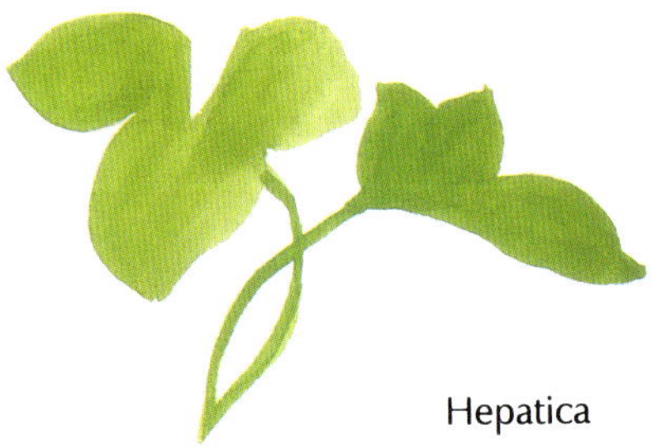

Hepatica

47. Along with the individual motifs, there is a rich array of second and scattered flowers available for the decoration of larger bouquets and to fill in white holes.

Decoration on the Glaze: Hunting Scenes

Motifs Chosen from Photos, Paintings or Nature Studies

We find hunting scenes painted on very early (early 18th century) Meissen pieces. The favorite pastime of the court elite quickly became a favorite subject of the painters. Hunting experiences of which one was proud, and which one wanted to remember, were also memorialized. At the same time, the first three-dimensional hunting portrayals were conceived, and in the form of figurines, trophies and other three-dimensional pieces, they constitute a considerable portion of Meissen production to this day.

Painting of hunting scenes was and still is defined naturalistically for the most part. When one takes the time to examine such a carefully painted service in peace and quiet, one sees clearly that all the smallest details were combined in the finest strokes. Thus there was created on every piece, with laborious effort, a painting in itself—often a true feast for the eyes.

For the dominant objects in a service, such as pitchers, tureens, salad bowls or meat platters, one usually chose lavishly composed scenes of hunting itself, or of wild animals in their natural surroundings. Here the portrayals of the larger animals are in their proper place. Since they fill up correspondingly large space and do not look lost on a large or extensive object (stags, deer, wild boars or the horses of the hunters). On the smaller pieces such as saucers, plates, soup bowls and many others, we naturally prefer to choose medium-sized motifs such as dogs, rabbits, or flocks of game birds.

Animals and hunters are almost always set in an appropriate landscape, such as is typical of the habitat of that type of wild animal. These segments of landscape—just like the portrayals of the animals—require very precise study of a model, which must then be copied (transferred) just as carefully. Here too, naturally, it is understood that one's own nature studies are really the best, since one thus gets acquainted with natural relationships better than from any photo, no matter how good.

As for the animals, though, it will not be possible for everyone to study the live subjects or be able to copy them, whether in the free world of nature or in the zoo. Here we can learn from good pictures in the literature of the subject. Trees and shrubs, on the other hand, can be studied and captured on the sketching pad almost everywhere.

The whole composition of a hunting scene is surely not simple, but can be learned by following certain rules. In simple terms, we have to combine large, medium-sized and small forms—similarly to flower painting. Naturally, this should all be done so that the effect of the picture is not "tipped" to one side by an overly large secondary motif, nor the picture made "one-sided" by unbalanced color concentration.

Good models for successful compositions can, of course, be found aplenty on pieces made in Meissen, but also on those of other brands that have used this subject. Only when oil paintings are used as models must great caution be applied in choosing a motif. I must admit that it is not easy to portray a group of deer or a stag in the morning dew of the woodlands without making a cliché of it, yet many examples show that it can be done. So don't have a stag "bell," but rather listen in the stillness of the early day. The coloring of the landscape painting should not be too colorful either, but—appropriate to the early morning hour—more of a gray-green, with a naturally pale-looking, foggy sky over the scene.

48. Nature studies from the author's sketch book. Try to make as many studies as you can. You learn the anatomy and movements of the animals and can later portray them convincingly. The sketches shown here were based on pictures by Rien Poortvliet.

Completing elements: Young animals, dogs, game birds, rabbits, medium-sized trees, bushes, small bridges or cabins.
Decorations: Hunting utensils such as guns, hunting horns, small game on the ground (pheasants, ducks).
Scattered bits: Twigs, mushrooms, flowers, but also a bullet pouch.

Small pieces (plates, saucers, vases, sugar bowls, milk pitchers and many more).
Main motifs: Young boars, ducks, partridges, pheasants, but also wild goats.
Other elements: Patches of grass, small bushes, nests, broken-off branches, stones, puddles.
Decoration and scattered bits: As above.

On the individual pieces of porcelain from earlier years are found very charmingly arranged groups of animals, that shine with a delicate color based on earth tones. Perhaps you know the works of Rien Poortvliet, the artist from Holland, who has created, in my view, the most beautiful hunting scenes and woodland motifs with dreamy but sure strokes. His sketches and nature studies can be a great help as models for us. Should you have the chance to examine porcelain with original painting, you can transfer all the contours of the motifs with a stencil.

In what follows, I would like to show, in a small array, several possibilities of combining animals, hunters, landscape elements and smaller details suitably in free composition.

Large pieces (meat platters, tureens, cake platters, coffeepots, wall plates, dinner plates, etc.).
Main motifs: Hunters on horseback, stags, elks, deer, large trees, sometimes buildings (hunting lodges).

The Painting Technique

Painting is done from the palette in flowing work processes. It is left to you to decide how much you can accomplish in the first step. Many a painter first applies a light basic color, on which, after it dries or is burned, work is continued. Others, though, apply most of the colors, wet on wet, and complete the picture by going over the whole of it again. As usual, what is important is that you mix all the ground colors in advance and apply them to the porcelain in the first application of paint. Why? Because several different layers of paint can cause additional problems in the burning, for they may burn off. It is better to mix the colors on the palette and then transfer them to the article you are painting.

Composition: Freehand and Stenciled

49. In his first year, a Meissen painting student begins to make anatomical studies, and after his four-year apprenticeship he spends the greatest amount of his free time expanding his knowledge as a painter of wildlife, so that he can utilize it some day.

First, thoroughly clean the piece with alcohol, in order to remove bits of dirt and grease from it. If you want to work out the motif to be painted just once, I recommend freehand drawing, since you spare yourself the work of making a stencil that way. Divide the surface to be painted into four equal segments by using a cross of string. This cross should also be applied to the pattern, so you can transfer the parts of the picture into the right quarters of it. If the size of the surface differs from that of the pattern, the latter can be enlarged or reduced with the help of a photocopier. Colored patterns are also preferable to black and white.

Now we draw all the necessary details on the porcelain (see also #53) with a very sharp Allstabilo pencil (such as no. 8008). Work out each quarter by itself, and sketch in the outlines of what is on the pattern. Small details, such as the folds in the clothes or the eyes of the hunters, can be left out for the time being. At first, only the clear outlines of the people, animals, trees and other objects are important. The string cross is a big help in terms of proportions, as it helps you to see how far each line reaches in each dimension of the painting. Do not let yourself be discouraged by a few mistaken lines, since such drawing requires a certain familiarity in using the drawing pencil. Any necessary correction is still possible, and with concentration and devotion to your work, you can attain the desired results in time. Should you ever really fail, the stencil still remains as a reliable tool.

Please apply this outline very lightly, so that you do not have too much graphite from the drawing pencil on the porcelain. During the first painting strokes, it could get into the lighter colors of the paint and spoil the whole impression. If it is possible, just draw one line per outline and avoid a heavy border. Should another line come too close, you can still make corrections with the small cotton

50. In the seventies, a variation of modern hunting painting was developed in Meissen; it could be painted in great detail as either on- or underglaze painting. Here you see several sketches that I made then to get acquainted with this new style of painting (#50-52).

51. An oak-leaf motif.

52. The rabbit motif was based on a nature calendar and was transferred and worked out with water colors.

swabs, that you can buy at the drugstore. To use them, dampen the cotton with a little alcohol. Many painters also use them to touch up the smallest areas. After you finish your drawing, check to see whether the whole motif is well balanced in the center and is not "off balance" to one side. To even it up, one can then add "counterweights" that were not on the original. Fill in the too sparse sections of the drawing with bushes or the like, and liven up a plain sky with a flock of birds—or clouds will do.

Now we want to have a somewhat closer look at the process of painting a medium-sized hunting scene. The main motif consists of two hunters on horseback, the stag, and the two large trees to the left and right, in order to make a frame for the picture. The picture is completed with the pack of hunting dogs, the stones and bushes. With the details of clothing and the formation of leaves and splashing water, the motif takes on added charm.

Applying the Paint

The paints on the palette—all the ones we need for the picture—are stirred with turpentine, as before any use. Since we are painting wet on wet, every detail of the picture has to be applied in the first work process. Choose a medium brush with a good point, which (as is often necessary) can still be trimmed. For the smallest details of the painting, such as faces, harness, clothing and pelts, you can keep a finer brush at hand, but it must lack any bristles that stick out to the side.

Where you begin to paint on the piece is not very important. In our example, we begin with the landscape, which encloses the whole picture and serves as a frame. To the left and right are large groups of trees, which give way to brighter bushes in the background and thus afford an impression of depth. Next to the big dead tree in the left foreground is a sand-colored bank of a stream, worked out especially carefully. The knotty, rotting structure of the tree can be worked out well in an initial stage, since the ocher-colored tones are lightly overlaid and varied gently with brown and yellow.

Use the paint in a somewhat pasty consistency, so the many nuances will have a longer time to mix into each other. A little drop of oil of cloves keeps the paint fresh, so the background can blend in with the foreground of the picture without problems. Naturally, one need not copy every stone and every bump in the ground exactly. It is more important that the observer gets the impression of a somewhat swampy ground surface, which is emphasized by the water nearby. In this part of the picture, a lot can be achieved by happenstance: that is, one goes over a brown-painted surface with lighter ocher to bring out light reflections, out of which a stone can be formed later. By the use of several colors, a picture is thus "put together" properly. But above all, remember the basic principle: Never paint anything finished! The last touches are applied when you pick out the details on the dry paint.

Next we turn to the trees at the right edge. You immediately see the different tone of the green and the touch of gray on the trunks (see #54). Therefore wash out the brush carefully and mix new colors on the glass palette. Do not paint the trunks and leaves too dark at the start, since this part of the picture would otherwise intrude too much into the center and optically challenge the main motif (riders and horses). The nearby bushes as well should only have the effect of a gentle green veil, with a few cloudy gray-blue tones worked into it. The green in the absolute center of the picture (directly behind the stag) may only let us presume that something is growing there. From these spots, where forest and sky meet, the motif takes on its depth (the bushes "go off to the rear," as the Meissen painter is in the habit of saying).

After this work process, check to see whether your painting as a whole is beginning to attract dust. If so, put it into the oven or electric stove right away and let it dry at 150 degrees Celsius. A word about drying in the electric stove. I am often asked when one should switch it on and off. My rule of thumb is to put the object in the cold oven, set it to 150 degrees, and then shut it off when the window in the front can still be touched with the hand. Then turn it off, open the door and let the piece cool off. But be careful! This does not apply to figures and pierced porcelain! These must be cooled with the oven door closed, since they would otherwise be exposed to overly great tensions.

Step-by-step Painting of a Dominant Part of the Picture

1st Step: Painting the figures and the water. Now we come to the really main motifs of our decoration. For the bodies of the animals, begin by using a soft gray tone, which can also be mixed with a little brown, and include the shadowed areas of muscles, ears, legs, etc., exactly like the pattern. Even at this early stage, the figures should express plasticity and movement. A precise copying of our studies or originals is essential—unless you are familiar with the anatomy of the animals through many of your own impromptu drawings. Stress the points that stand out, such as the nose, eyes, hooves and other such parts to be portrayed strongly, and only then complete the soft, moving parts such as tails or sections of pelts. Treat the riders in the same way: first paint their black hats, their hair, their swords, and then the saddles and harness. The brown tones of a stag, a horse and two dogs should now be applied.

For the natural portrayal of water, in which the entire event takes place, the first phase should be bright and striped. Only later, in the finishing stage, do we mix blue-violet, gray and green, in order to achieve a dirtier shade, such as stirred-up, muddy water would have.

In general, it is best to use dull earth colors to portray all the scenery, forming individual points of light with the hunters' uniform jackets. There is also light for the foreground, which can be brightened with a light yellow. Bluish reflections of the dogs in the water can also be added later.

Now the entire motif should dry thoroughly. If necessary, one can do an intermediate burning, a low burning temperature of about 600 degrees Celsius is enough to fix the color and thus keep it dust-free.

2nd Step: The Main Process. Here you should begin with the tree at the left front. Along with the shore, it forms the foreground and therefore stands out particularly. The realistic bark and the branches are reproduced very precisely and, like the ground in front, finished in a brownish-yellow tone. In the finished painting, seen in #54, you can see how this complete segment stands by itself through this nuance of color. This coloring does not appear anywhere else in the painting, so that the foreground is clearly separated from the center and the background.

The central area is dominated by the blue-green tone of the water, contrasting with the contours of the animals. The white horse of one hunter, on the other hand, was placed in the light before a dark background by the painter—as one sees, a carefully conceived and balanced composition of the whole scene.

First finish painting the animals in the center of the picture. Fine lines define the masses of the limbs, heads, antlers and eyes. Only after that come the soft tones of the hair and muscles. Copy the darker areas exactly as in the pattern: a gray dog is set off well by its light contours from the dark brown of the stag's hair. During the painting, you should also try to determine how the painter has achieved many special effects. This will be a big help later, when you are transferring your own designs.

The two riders also demand a great deal of ability and patience when you work out the details of their uniform folds. It is not an easy task to create a convincing appearance of cloth on such small surfaces. The most important rule is not to make these places look dead! If you put in too much detail, then the light has disappeared, and in any case, there are areas of color that only look darker in shadow and make a perspective effect impossible. Thus paint the clothing lightly and let the white of the plate provide the lightness. After painting on the shadows, these white areas will be covered with the appropriate tones and will then shine brightly at the eye of the beholder (#54). This method also guarantees that even after highlighting, details like sleeves, collars, buttons and other details remain clearly recognizable.

For even greater plasticity, one can sometimes use white to set off details. Harness, belts, buckles and even sword-hilts then look elegant "on" the painting. After application, the white is covered with the appropriate color.

Faces and hands should appear in one flesh tone. This should be attained by applying light red tones to the porcelain extremely thinly. For this use, try the flower red from the palette. One can usually use it when it has been thinned considerably with enough creamy painting oil (don't use thick oil!). Naturally, there are also ready-mixed flesh colors on the market, but one should test them in advance. Among them, there are tones that react very differently when they are burned. Sometimes they come out of the oven glowing so strongly that they are really not suitable for faces.

Now we mix the finishing paint for the water, as mentioned before, from rather dull, gray nuances. Near the banks and under the dogs we add the shadows with unsteady pressure, simultaneously giving the wetness its "glowing lights". Off to the middle of the picture, these pressures become fewer and fewer, losing themselves in the background.

Next, the big trees in the right background are finished. They are not to be painted in such a filigree manner as the tree in the left foreground, and have more of an effect as forms than as pictures. Two broad trunks, which take on movement only from a little bark structure, and another two evergreen trees, which swing into the center of the picture with their green color. Restrain yourself very much when painting the bushes at the right edge of the picture: light gray-green shadows are all you need. Even less paint is needed for the patch of woods that disappears in the absolute background (behind the stag).

Now just one important tip about color: In landscape painting, try not to use any pure black, if possible. Even the very deep tones of stones and tree trunks should be created with a mixture of dark blue-gray-brown tones. Thus you avoid hardness, such as is not found in nature. Without black, the overall impression of the landscape remains soft and natural.

3rd Step: Finishing Work. Now that all the individual segments of the decoration have been finished, we come to a check of the overall impression. It may well be that one or another gently painted spot is not satisfactory and must be strengthened with one more coat of paint. If, for example, the water in our picture were painted too bright, it would look as if the animals were moving without having ground beneath their feet. In such a case, it is best to add a more or less heavy coat over the area in question and thus finish the picture. Also, if there are small white flecks, that should not be present, standing out here and there (perhaps in the animals' bodies or the shadows of the trees), a touch of paint will help.

The finishing touches can also include highlighting details with setting-off white. These include the smallest leaves of the dark bunches of leaves, or fine sprays of water in the places where the dogs are running in the water. In patches of meadow, small flowers can also be suggested with white, which "shine like pearls" brightly amid the green.

Compare the pattern and the painting once more to make sure they agree, and then quickly put the piece in the oven, so that these rather large areas of paint do not attract dust unnecessarily. In the burning itself, on account of the many mixings, now and then nuances can be created quite by chance. But this very happening makes the painting your most original work. When the work is finished, one should not compare the model and the painting endlessly and get annoyed about variations. For not only have we become inspired by a master from times past, but he too had his models in some other work or in nature itself, and gave the work his own signature—just as we have done.

53. A fine pencil outline of the basic shapes of a hunting motif (see description in text, page 52).

54. The finished decoration. The description of the work is on page 56.

Decoration On the Glaze : Wild Fruits

The painting of woodland fruits is a genre of decoration found rather rarely, and can really be regarded as a subgroup of fruit painting in general—just like water vegetation or vegetable motifs. Thanks to their naturalistic reproduction and sometimes glowing colors, woodland fruits can be very appetizing to see, and they enjoy great popularity, particularly among those who love the world of nature.

These decorative motifs are primarily suitable for porcelain pieces that find their home in the kitchen or the dining room. But restaurants that feature wild products on their menu, or rustic hunting lodges, are also suitable places to utilize such motifs, whether on dishes or in room decorations.

Woodland fruit painting is usually done on individual pieces such as wall plates, sugar bowls, candy dishes or the like. I myself have already decorated complete sets of coffee or dinner dishes with this painting; the coffee dishes were to show fruits that could also be used in cake (such as blueberries, wild strawberries and the like). Mushrooms should be reserved for paintings on dinner table dishes.

In principle, only edible berries and mushrooms should be painted (a bright-colored Amanita mushroom can, as an exception to the rule, look very nice when painted, perhaps, on a child's plate as a "house" for dwarfs), when an appetizing appearance is desired. There are goodly numbers of very tasty mushrooms which, alas, look rather unappealing with their grayish-blue coloring. So stick with the well-known and nice-looking types such as the Boletus, browncap, butter mushroom, chestnut mushroom, champignon and others. This also applies to our berries. Thus as colorful as the barberry is, its toxicity automatically excludes it from our purposes.

The following list is meant to make it easier for you to make the right choice and create large and small fruit arrangements.

Large fruits as the central motif (similar to the main flowers in a bouquet): Any of the larger and more colorful edible mushrooms, walnuts, chestnuts, wild quinces, wild crabapples, medlar, and many more.

Medium fruits to fill out a motif (similar to the binding and subsidiary flowers in a bouquet): Small mushrooms, acorns, blackberries, raspberries, wild strawberries, then hazel nuts, juniper, elderberries, bilberries, cranberries, wild grapes, cherries and others.

Small twigs and grasses to brighten up (connectors): Heather, wild vetch, hawthorn, stoneberries, mealberries, white thorn and others.

55. Various wild fruits.

Painting Fruits on Concave and Flat Surfaces

Arranging wild fruits decoratively calls for a somewhat different conception than arranging flowers. While flowers usually "sway" freely on the porcelain, the wild fruits are enclosed in a frame of grass or leaves. The whole motif becomes more compact and heavy, since a fruit, like a fleshy mushroom, expresses considerably more corporeality than an airy, almost weightless flower. Therefore large, weighty wild fruits (such as a large mushroom) belong in the center of the motif! Smaller mushrooms or a few acorns can fill out the picture, and a few twigs with small blossoms can finish it off. A few examples of such designs are shown on pages 60 and 61.

A "white" flower is also very useful in any large still life. It projects itself very nicely "in front of" the painting through its bright coloring (soft purple and blue) and thus creates plasticity and depth. But make the field around such a flower dark deliberately, in order to increase the optical impression that it is projecting out of the background. In addition, the flower should not border on the white of the porcelain anywhere, so that it stands out the more clearly.

Smaller scattered elements can be raised from the whole motif; for example, small berries and leaves. But insects, various butterflies and the like, are also very suitable. With the right arrangement, the observer gets the impression that they are fluttering lightly and playfully over the motif.

When painting, pay strict attention to the precise shaping of the individual fruits. Many mushrooms have a very typical shape and must be reproduced in that form (for example, the chanterelle). A stencil, with which one can copy very lovely fruits out of an appropriate pattern book, is, as usual, a big help in doing this, Naturally, one's own nature studies, that one makes with self-collected mushrooms and fruits, are even more valuable. It makes a difference whether one paints fruits from a photo or stencil or holds them in one's hand and thus can study them from every possible angle.

The same thoroughness in formation applies to the many shades of green in the forest. Both the form and the color have to be chosen well to achieve the naturalistic impression of the painting. One can make the greenery look even more interesting by painting it in autumn colors. Purple borders and golden yellow glazes give the whole picture a splendidly colorful impression. In the two examples on page 62, the colorful leaves even become the main motif—a brilliant reproduction of the fireworks found in the woods every year. These two plates are old Meissen pieces and are still painted today on order.

The Painting Technique

Paintings of wild fruits are made by using the hole palette. The paints are kept fresh with a little oil of cloves and stirred daily. In this type of work, the dotting brush is very important. All the soft surfaces, such as large leaves, mushroom caps or fruits, are dotted. For this we need up to three different sizes of brush (4, 7 and 12 mm). The daily cleaning of the brushes goes without saying.

The division of colors is the same as in flower painting: two thirds are fruit colors, one third is the green of the leaves. Now and then, you can also portray a cut fruit, or one that has been gnawed on by an animal. This heightens the naturalistic effect. Paint the stems and branches in earth color tones, and make the fruits very glowing. But avoid manneristic elements when you paint, as we have learned from Meissen flower painting: that means you should not always use the same color in different places in individual painting sequences, but unite the entire composition through the use of wet-on-wet painting.

57, 58. Colorful autumn leaves and wild fruits from Meissen, circa 1880.

59. Sketches and color tests of wild berries and leaf shapes.

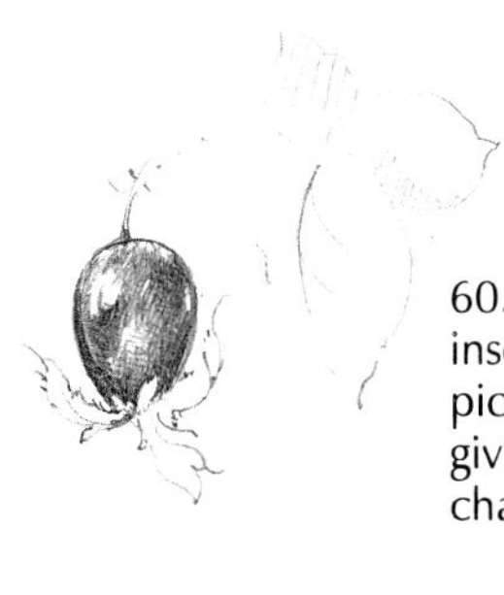

60. Composition studies of mushrooms and fruits as well as insects, which can be used in scattered form to lighten up a picture. The little insects are mostly imaginary, with soft colors giving them that shimmering appearance that makes them so charming.

61. A lovely, colorful still life with a large mushroom in the center, smaller ones beside it, and delicate twigs and grasses to decorate the spaces.

Decoration On the Glaze : Landscapes and Buildings

This chapter was added to the book on the requests of many who paint houses, since in the first volume, "Porcelain Painting," I had regarded it as for beginners and thus only offered very small examples of it.

Step-by-step Painting on a Wall Plate

Now we are going to turn to a really demanding task, and choose as our subject nothing less than the symbol of Meissen—the Cathedral on Albrecht's Hill—for a large painting that will fit well on a wall plate of 23 cm diameter. I have very deliberately expanded the painting process from three to six steps, so that the course of work on this very finely detailed motif can be carried out with precision.

1st Step (#62): The outline is laid out on the plate, which has been cleaned with alcohol, and as usual, the two familiar choices of freehand drawing or stencil have been available. Since one paints such a lavish picture rarely, as a rule, and then only as a single piece, freehand drawing surely saves the most time. But if one can reckon on reorders, one should take the trouble to make a stencil, which can be put to use quickly, and which will guarantee numerous pieces a similarly qualitative composition.

In all your work, make sure that the main motif (in this case the cathedral) is never in the middle of the picture, but off to one side. The cross of string on the plate can be a big help in orientation here too, making a clear division easier. Another unwritten law is that the horizon line must never lie right in the middle of the plate. It has a boring effect when such a round painted surface appears to have been divided in half, as if with a ruler. At best, 2/3 sky is balanced by 1/3 ground (see our example).

As a pattern for your picture, choose a sharp motif that shows all contours and shadows clearly and is also not too bright or dull in terms of color. It goes without saying that a postcard cannot be an adequate model—photos in good photo albums are far better.

When making the outline with the Allstabilo pencil, one must again be careful not to get lost in details: too many graphite lines on the plate can disturb the colors later, when you paint. First just outline the buildings, the lines of roofs, walls and bushes with clear basic lines; details such as tiles, gutters and chimneys can be left off at first.

For the sky, one should usually do without a pattern, for dark pencil lines would only detract. The cloudy, moving restlessness of the sky can be achieved much more easily by applying the paint mixed with turpentine in a variety of directions and attaining an interesting effect by chance. You should also make the sky a little more stormy than it is in pictures in books—a glowing blue surface over two thirds of the motif would look too much like a picture postcard sent by a vacationer.

2nd Step (#63): Now we begin to lay out the entire motif with a dark but soft drawing color (purple mixed with gray). You can start now to add small shadings by windows and roof cornices. The interesting play of light and shadow on the church steeples can now be painted exactly like the model. Special care is needed here to make sure that the entire picture is enlivened by the optical effect of the cathedral. On the surfaces that later provide the areas of greenery, you can also begin to lay out the lighter shadows. But be careful! Don't let them get too dark, for these areas will be painted with dark green later.

For the sky, we then apply the first light blue-gray tones that indicate the positions of the clouds. Use the paint more thick than thin, so that you can work it later with the dotting brush. But first, use a broad brush to mix in the tone suggested by the photo. With the brush, when washed out in turpentine, one can also pick out white clouds from the paint that is there.

3rd Step (#64): Once you have slowly but surely covered the whole picture with soft colors, the first clear, hard shadows can be applied, already providing clear plasticity and perspective. This also includes the emphasizing of individual lines. For the wall sections of the houses, you can paint the colorful washes and the various colors of the roof materials according to the model. The roofs of the Albrechtsburg were newly redone in the socialistic era, at very varied times, and thus not matching, so that we are looking at a very varied mixture of gray slate, red tiles and the green verdigris of the copper roofs.

4th Step (#65): All the areas of greenery in the picture are now covered with cloudy green colors. Begin now to add the first blue-green tree shadows to the wet paint of the undercoat, and paint the individual leaves on the twig at right too, making them very clear against the already dried sky blue.

Now all the areas not yet painted receive their chosen colors. Try to come very close to the final nuances of color that you want, so that at the end you do not have to do too much all over again, which would make the layer of paint too thick (and risk its coming off during burning!). The steeples are now accentuated with a green-gray tone, even though in nature they are more blackish. As already noted, the pure color of black is to be avoided and replaced by a dark gray, mixed with dark blue or brown.

5th Step (#66): The less experienced painter should apply an intermediate burning before starting the last two work steps. This way, one can analyze the first paint reactions in the oven and take steps to improve them.

Now the greenery in the picture gets its full treatment. Apply the areas of shadow, according to the model, in the right places. For these corners, mix the cool shadow tones by adding some blue-green or purple to the green. Bright washes for places that lie in the light can be painted in yellow-green. Fine details of the buildings, such as window frames, chimneys and other roof details can also be added. To what extent you want to detail a roof is naturally up to you, but it should never be forgotten that our main motif is the cathedral, and nothing around it should take attention away from it. So do not make every roof tile in the foreground recognizable, which would be a distraction. The sky can also be made livelier now; this decision too is yours to make.

6th Step (#67): This consists of going over the entire picture one last time, perhaps even adding a little wash.

62-67. Creation of the "Cathedral on the Albrechtsburg in Meissen" motif in six individual steps (see also the directions in the text, pp. 66-67).

62. Outline

63. Fine preliminary color work.

64. Addition of the first shadows.

65. Addition of the green and colored washes.

66. Addition of fine details.

67. The finished painting "Cathedral on the Albrechtsburg in Meissen".

Decoration On the Glaze: Purple Indian Decor

To meet the requests of many of my readers, I would like to deal briefly in this book with the formation of Indian decorations as well. To be sure, step-by-step directions are not needed, as the basic technique (stenciling—drawing—stamping—overpainting) always remains the same. So we shall concentrate on a single type of Indian decoration typical of Meissen work, the Indian green, which can also be done in purple.

This extremely decorative painting has enjoyed lasting popularity for centuries among porcelain fans. Surely the glowing liveliness of these stylized plants and flower ornaments contributes much to it. A table lavishly ornamented with it is tremendously impressive, since the fine-lined drawing of the individual segments in their totality has a really elegant effect. Every part is also ornamented with the typical decorative border, and the use of powdered gold, with its heavy effect, adds more value to the complete work.

This decoration was formerly painted in a very free and loose style, and on old Meissen porcelain one sees a flowing type of painting. But since one has stabilized the pattern on every piece by using a stencil, a very disciplined painting is guaranteed. Many critics of Indian painting, of course, have rejected this painfully precise use of pen and brush, because as they see it, the personal note of the painter seen in hand-painting is completely missing. In the majority of pieces, one sees very clearly how light and soft the drawing pen was used, all the same. Then even a piece from a service, with a repeated motif, becomes an unmistakable individual piece.

Making the Stencil and the Design

For this decoration it is difficult to give a set of rules for the initial drawing, since in Meissen all the stencils for all the possible components are ready for the painter, and we in the realm of hobbies can really start off with original pieces of our own designs. For the different sizes of plate, we can enlarge or shrink the pattern given here by using a photocopier.

The great number of patterns for concave areas must nevertheless be copied with tissue paper, with some trouble, from porcelain pieces that we find in the possession of friends or acquaintances or in collections. The motif can be copied onto the milk-white transparent paper more easily when one puts a thin layer of alcohol between the porcelain and the paper, to make the lines of the painting easier to see. This paper stencil is transferred in the usual way to lead foil and fitted to the object to be painted.

Purple Indian Decor

Here we have one main rosette down in the center, around which all the other details are grouped. At the left and right there are finely branched segments with many kinds of flowers and leaves. On curved pieces, such as cups, we put the rosette in the center of the outer cup surface (opposite the handle) and have the other small patterns running to the left and right of it, so that they reach around to the handle. Naturally, a part of the decoration has to be left out, since there is not as much space on a cup as on a significantly larger plate. Have a quiet look around the porcelain sections of the department stores some time, and make sketches, or even better, photos, if they let you. Often specific painting patterns can be used for several shapes. Thus the stencil for a cup might also fit nicely on the lower part of a sugar bowl, or the stencil for a coffeepot could be used for a vase of similar size.

Drawing Lines

The borders of the purple or green painting should be drawn freehand. For such thin lines you do not need a stencil, and you can paint quickly with an Allstabilo pencil. On rounded parts, the lines are almost always on the diminishing areas of the form (see also #91, 92), except on pieces with lids. On our plate example, the border consists of three thin lines that follow the curving rim of the plate at differing intervals (see #71). It is easy to imagine how practiced one must be to paint such a line with the drawing pen, always at the same distance from the edge.

With just one tool—a potter's wheel—and by using a border brush, and being patient, one can have more chance of success. The plate is centered on the turning surface and carefully set in motion. The brush, well filled with paint, can now be put down at a place of your choice, and a stripe will follow the curve of the plate's rim. Take the brush away when the paint in the stripe becomes too light, and dip it in the paint again. For this work you have to have a lot of patience. On your first attempts you may not have the right motion, or the paint on the brush may run out in the middle of the line. Then again, the space between the line and the rim, or the next stripe, may not be right—there are many chances to make mistakes.

To these lines, small double lines in triangular form are added, between which the gold dots are placed, but first they have to be painted with green drawing color. More about a smooth process is coming. When you want to work your way into the fine striping technique and line acrobatics of Indian painting, it cannot hurt to begin with some simple decorations. An ideal pattern for the beginner is the so-called three-leaf motif (also Indian painting with gold spots and border). It is not as multi-leaved as the pattern described below, and as a result it is simpler to accomplish, since it is easier to handle. Now here is the exact sequence of our green Indian painting for #71.

Step-by-step Painting on a Plate

1st Step (#68): On the cleaned plate, the motif is transferred with rubbed drawing charcoal or drawn freehand; missing bits are filled in with the Allstabilo pencil. The border is drawn freehand. At each end of the imagined string cross is a small rosette between the lines.

2nd Step (#69): With the chosen green paint, all the lines are now drawn. Try to match the original color as best you can, in order to base it on the Meissen ground color. The drawing and touching stamps are painted in a rather dark chromium oxide green, while a very light wash is put over it. You must master the work with the drawing pen very well, since the Indian technique requires a high degree of drawing ability, and we must create a wide variety of arches, curves and rosette outlines. Capable use of the pen makes the job very much easier.

3rd Step (#70): Into the well-dried drawing we now set the stamps with the brush. These are the small dark areas that we can discover in every leaf. Sometimes larger, sometimes smaller, they give a certain strength to the painting and yet make the relatively strict drawing somewhat "softer". For them, the same green as used in drawing will be used, but put on somewhat thinner, since it should not flow so fluidly out of the pen, but is applied with a medium-sized brush. For this work process, study the model very carefully, since we have not stenciled the stamps and must add them freehand.

4th Step (#71): The drawing shows us the completely applied overlay of green, which was painted on the leaves evenly and lightly everywhere in the motif. Here too, please pay strict attention to the model, so that you do not also paint the areas for the gold by mistake. Last of all, the powdered gold will be set very carefully into the places that we have left white.

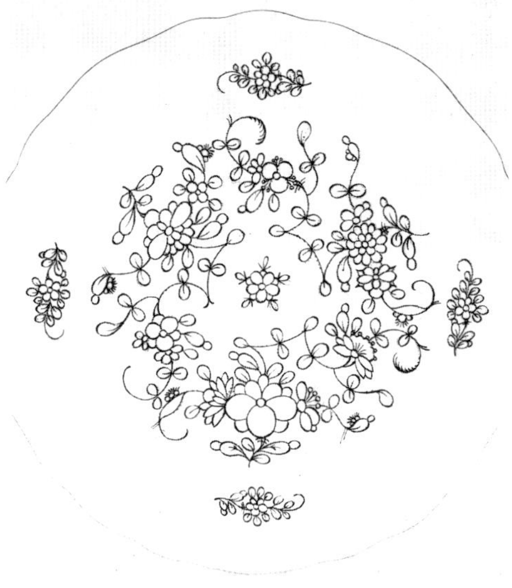

68-71. Green Indian painting in four steps.

68. The stenciled basic outline.

69. The first brush work and the decorated border. For the lines, see the text on page 69.

70. Setting the spots of color.

71. Adding the green overlay.

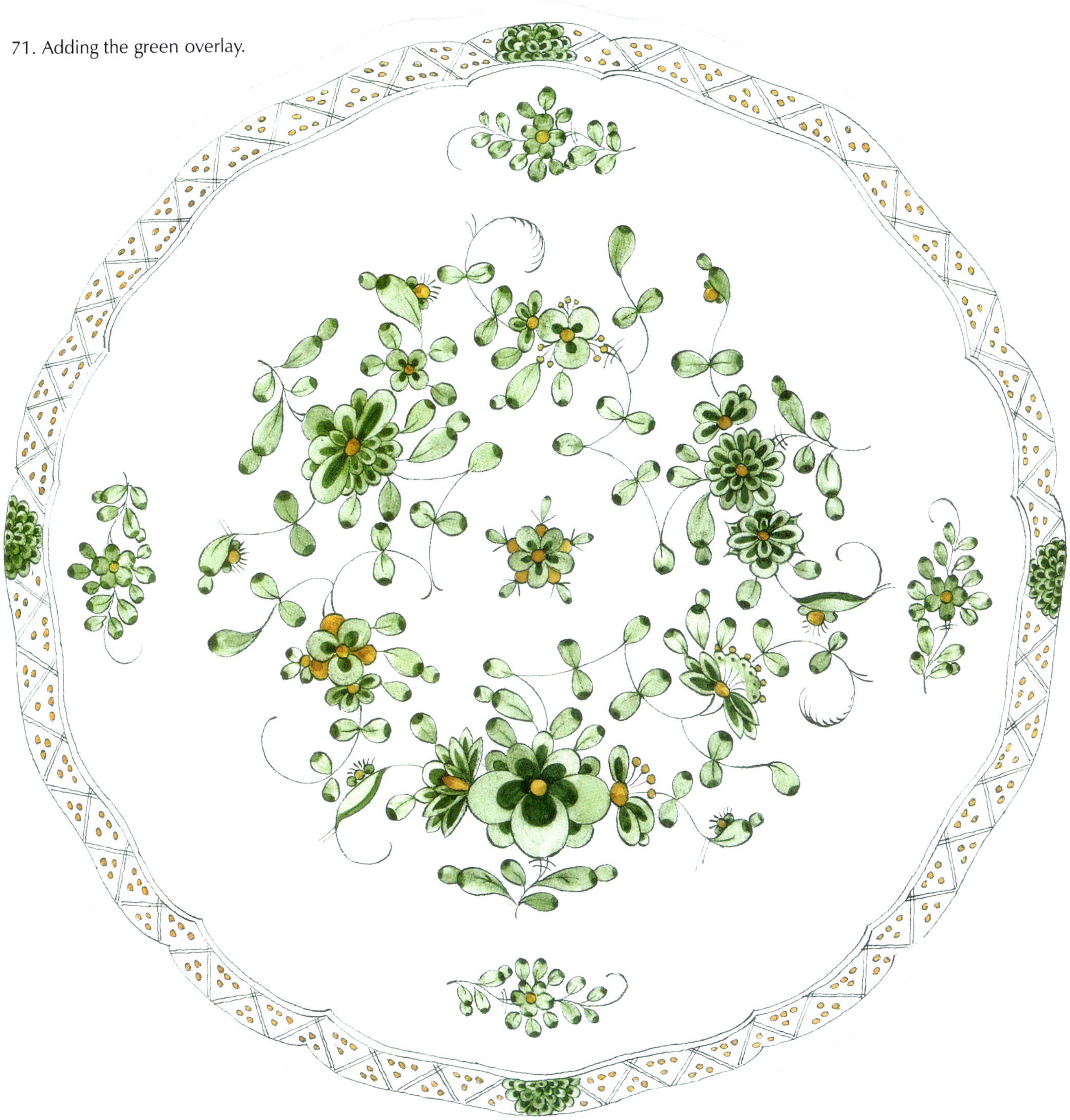

Decoration On the Glaze: Onion Pattern

The Meissen onion pattern ranks among the most traditional of all porcelain decorations. Since it appeared in the year 1740, it has been made in countless variations—the fact that a real "onion-pattern pestilence" has been spoken of lets us know how popular and widespread this pattern was and is. In addition, there are great numbers of possible origins of this pattern, but its origin from Asia, or more precisely from China, seems fairly certain. Naturally, in this decoration the portrayal of pomegranates, peaches or citrus fruits—mandarin oranges were also included—and the fact that mandarins were not known in Europe at that time may have resulted in its being taken for an onion there. There is a great deal of literature on the developmental history of this pattern, but here we want to follow the development of the pattern on the porcelain and understand the secret of its harmony.

Symbolism and Pattern Variations

The onion pattern takes its attractive power from its perfect ornamental structure, which we perceive in its harmony only unconsciously. On the originally round plates (before the origin of the so-called "Neuer Ausschnitt" or "new cut"), there are eight fruits on the raised flange. Four pomegranates and four peaches form an octagon. Right in the middle is the "perfected human being," portrayed both by a bamboo stem and a bamboo blossom as a masculine symbol. To its right are mixed symbolic flowers, chrysanthemums and lotus blossoms, as the feminine symbol. The Western theory of life also uses the onion pattern as a model for the exemplary layered existence of mankind in the eternal process of becoming and departing. The fact that the coloring is essentially blue is surely explained by the fact that this sky color, even in Greek and Roman mythology, was the color of the gods of Olympus, whether Zeus and Hera or Juno and Jupiter. The princes of the eighteenth century also chose this color very deliberately as an expression of their—ordained by heaven—worldly power.

As early as 1888, the Meissen factory felt compelled to protect "their" onion pattern by adding swords in the bamboo stem, since at that time every imaginable manufacturer was copying the onion pattern more or less well. The addition of the swords guarantees the original Meissen origin to the customer. An imitation of this trade mark and protected pattern is therefore, as already noted, also forbidden the hobby painter as regards the onion pattern and several Indian designs.

Unlike the decoration from the Meissen factory, our pieces are made with the over-glaze technique, which makes them look different for this reason alone. For a short time, though, the well-known pattern was painted on the glaze in Meissen too, and, in fact, in purple. When I saw this variety for the first time, I immediately thought of a work that could have been made outside the factory. My instructor, though, explained the true situation to me, and I must say that this color version pleases me very much. The pattern seems clearer, more graphic and, all in all, very neat. There is also a combination of the onion pattern in which the underglaze painting is completed later with over-glaze elements. This, though, is a matter of taste, and there are not a few who say that the piece thus decorated looks overloaded; on the other hand, there are also fans who only find the onion pattern meaningful thus—such as when the blue underglaze lines are embellished with over-glaze red and the right amount of gold.

In addition, I would like to make you aware of a third type of work, which is painted using the over-glaze technique and looks like underglaze work. This involves "sharp-fire" painting and in-glaze painting. Both are painted on the glazed piece and take on a soft, blurry appearance thanks to a high burning temperature. A layman can scarcely see differences from underglaze decoration. These paints can also be recommended for other patterns, since they create an impression very much like water colors.

The Formation

The preparation of a piece with the onion pattern is like that of the Indian painting. The stencil gives us the contours that later must be applied with paint and partly colored. Here, as opposed to underglaze painting, we have the advantage of not having to work so fast, since our piece is not as raw and absorbent as an unglazed object. Perhaps you have seen at the Meissen factory display how quickly the blue painter's hands have to apply the onion pattern so that at the end of a line there is no dot left because the brush was left on the porcelain too long. Naturally this is above all a question of routine, and during training it takes several months before the trainee is able to master the smooth line painting that is required for the onion pattern. The fact that all the lines are painted with the brush and not the pen makes for a further difficulty—but there is no other way to handle underglaze painting, and even in our over-glaze variation the lines have to have a certain minimum strength that can be attained better with the brush.

72. The onion pattern on a plate. The lotus flower is shown at upper right, with the bamboo stem in the center. The crossed swords below are not to be copied, as they are a protected trade mark.

73. For comparison, a milk pitcher in plain white and one decorated with the onion pattern.

The purple over-glaze painting is shown completed on pages 91 and 92. For a better total impression, I again show a medium-sized plate, since all the portions of the decoration can be seen on it. This type of onion pattern was available around 1900, but it was not painted very often. Therefore pieces from this era and in this style can safely be regarded as rarities, which cannot be said of the blue pieces—quite the opposite.

For our purple painting we use two tones of color, which we have already met in the Indian painting: a dark drawing purple for the contours and a light (not too rosy!) shade for shadings on the stem and on the flowers and fruits on the rim of the plate.

Here too, the exact pattern should be taken from pattern drawings, which you can get from books, catalogs or your own photos. It is best, of course, to make a pattern directly from an original Meissen piece. The trained hobby painter, who already has several years of experience, will surely paint the decoration freehand. On flat surfaces, the string cross will be a big help; and the curved parts show a repeating symmetry. The middle section (bamboo stem and double leaf) is centered on the plate. At the left, the branches with the bamboo flowers spread out, and at the right is the curve with chrysanthemum and lotus flowers. On the back and side areas of many curved sections are scattered forget-me-nots. The large pomegranate rim is left out of some curved areas for lack of space as well as because of the optical effect, and replaced by a simple ribbon edge. In this pattern too, one can easily apply the pattern used on a certain piece to others, as long as they are similar in form and size (for example, saucers and bowl lids).

Should you still have problems in shadowing unburned contours, put the pieces in question in the oven first and fix the paint lightly to the glaze at 760 degrees Celsius before you go on with the painting. The fine lines from the border of the central section to the rim of the plate are completed with the edging brush on the wheel. When all the bright-colored paints have been applied according to the pattern, the article is given its final burning.

74. Several types of scattered flowers for the onion pattern, done in blue. They are ideal decorative elements on lids, handles and feet of porcelain pieces.

75. The work process for the onion pattern in over-glaze technique. Upper half: the entire motif is applied with rubbed charcoal and a stencil.
Lower half: all the shapes are applied with the brush, in drawing purple. A pen drawing would do it too, but always looks rather runny and especially thin.

76. The fields are filled out with bright purple. The small arch in the bamboo trunk is left empty, or could hold the artist's initials.

77. The border and the pattern below show possibilities of making the onion pattern look different without losing its typically Chinese character.

78. While the saucer of the coffee service has only a small rim border (see page 73, lower left), the kitchen plate (diameter 91 cm) has a sufficiently broad rim to hold the decorative pomegranate border.

79. On a big platter of 43 cm length, the handle bows as well as the onion pattern are painted a glowing underglaze blue. Through the somewhat "cloudy" application of the blue, this ribbon appears even more mobile.

80. A look at a fancy table service with pierced rim. All the members of the rim plait are decorated and give the filigreed rim a beneficial symmetry.

Decoration On the Glaze : Grapevines

The Meissen grapevine is scarcely less familiar than the onion pattern. Everyone knows the rims of almost blackish-green leaves that encircle the most varied pieces of chinaware in great variety. They are always shown as an endless circle, just as if they had been plaited onto a ring. On a lavishly decorated table, this strictly geometrical arrangement of the decoration provides a contrast and an extraordinary charm. The grapevine leaves, often mistakenly described as gillyflower leaves, are (like the onion pattern) painted at Meissen by using the underglaze technique, of course. What many people do not know, though, is that the leaves are copied with a stencil and not at all drawn individually. In addition, the same shapes always appear at regular intervals on a painted piece, which is explained by the fact that such a stencil, as a transfer pattern, is used several times on a plate or bowl. A plate ring can thus be formed out of three or four individual segments.

Making the Stencil

These stencils are naturally an ideal source of help in the production of whole series, as is customary in Meissen. In the hobby world, their preparation is only recommended when you are preparing a whole coffee service or already know that you are going to paint the same decoration again in the future. With these stencils, incidentally, only the outlines of the green leaves are cut out. The black stems and leaf ribs are added freehand. But let's take it one step at a time.

Choose a firm piece of not too thick posterboard or a similar material. Through the many points on the leaves in the decoration, the stencil should stand out with really sharp-cut angles—it is best to make them using a hard material not too prone to absorption.

The grapevine decoration can also be used very effectively in the over-glaze technique for private purposes. After all, it will scarcely be possible for most non-professional painters to find sources of supply for unglazed porcelain—and then too, the high first burning of the underglaze is better done by an expert.

Color and Arrangement of the Grapevines

An over-glaze grapevine looks no less interesting when the nuances of green color are well made. The practiced amateur painter can easily mix this typical green tone, and after a few test burns will surely be successful. But I have also seen strange-colored grapevine paintings that were quite charming. For the right touch of color you should always have a genuine Meissen piece lying beside your work for direct comparison. The Meissen green is unusually deep and yet strongly radiates warmth. Through its location under the glaze, it also takes on a particular kind of softness that cannot be attained on top of the glaze. The deepness of the green is so strong that, even at just a slight distance, one can no longer make out the black ribs of the leaves. For the "stemming" of the leaves we choose a neutral black from our flower palette.

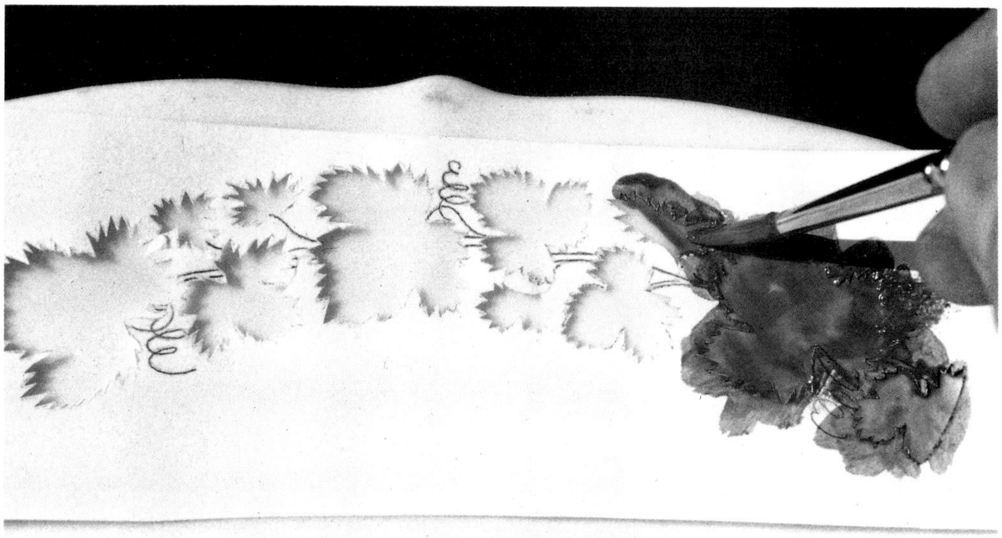

81-83. Making the stencil for the grapevine decor, applying it to the porcelain and painting over it, with the finished motif below.

a

84. The color of the green grapevine.

b

c

85, 86. The "modern" grapevine painting with grapes in the faintest pale green.

The precise arrangement of the leaves can be studied best from an original piece, but can also be composed freely. It is basically nothing more than a matter of a few variations of leaves in different sizes. Sometimes they are portrayed from above, and sometimes from the side. A repeating symmetry dominates. You can, of course, also take the exact shapes from the original piece onto transparent paper and copy them onto the stencil. The cutting itself is best done by hand with a small scalpel. With it, one can cut cleanly into the sharp points of the shapes and produces clear, neat contours which later make smooth painting possible. Well-cut zigzags on the leaves are also necessary, in order to avoid touching up afterward. It would be very burdensome and time-consuming if we had to correct the shapes of all the little leaves after everything else was done.

Once the stencils are very neatly cut, we still have to bend and press them here and there to fit them to the piece in question. For big, convex pieces, such as soup tureens, it is advisable to use a softer stencil material. I have even heard of painters who have used a flexible airbrush foil. The results are not known to me, but I can imagine that the material tears when removed from the piece after painting. But there is also a very slightly adhesive foil (available in a roll) that is well suited to use for painting stencils and is widely used in advertising.

Composition of the Pattern

The porcelain coloring should be rubbed on quite thick and creamy for the coating. Among the underglaze painters in Meissen, a water-soluble paint is used which, brushed on really thick, is sucked up quite "hungrily" by the raw, unglazed porcelain. Thus a sufficiently thick coat of paint can be applied quickly, and the color tone is right too. For our work with over-glaze paints, though, we must generally put on several layers of paint. But be careful! Do not put it on too thick, otherwise the layer can come off while burning.

The deepness of the green should be attained by mixing the paints and not by the heaviness of the paint. But add a drop of oil of cloves to make the leaf surfaces look very quiet and self-contained. The oil of cloves, as is known, makes sure that the mixture of paint "works" a little while drying and spreads out the particles of paint evenly. Should the grapevine leaves have become somewhat uneven anyway, they can be painted over after drying. If the cross of leaves is applied to one piece in one process, then a longer drying time is required.

In addition, when you apply the green paint, use a sufficiently large brush, so that the surface does not have to be touched up, which could cause striping. A wide, soft squirrel-hair brush, such as is used, for example, in sculpture to dust off figures, is ideally suited. A particularly pointed tip is not necessary, since it must essentially just take up enough paint. Thus you want a brush with a lot of "body". Naturally, the situation is otherwise as regards the drawing brush for the stems and leaf veins. Here a high-quality flower-painting brush, cut out as much as possible afterward, is advisable. With it, we first paint the main stem of the vine, which holds the motif together like a ring. When you look at a Meissen piece, you will see that it runs straight through the leaves and thus gives support to the whole motif. As for color, it is painted the same color as the leaves.

Now it is time to pick out the details with black. To be sure, the green background must be sufficiently dried or even burned before one can begin with this. At first each grape leaf is given its three central veins, which are then amplified with fine, very straight branches. Then the leaves are attached. So that they do not hang freely in the air, we draw fine lines from every leaf to the main vine. To the vine itself we add fine points (not thorns!) and small tendrils, which naturally help the vines to climb. These tendrils, which are quite lumpy in nature, are therefore painted by us to look a little more graceful and thus more elegant.

In closing, the rims, knobs, handles, spouts and other parts of the individual pieces are finished, that is, painted. This is done only with the green of the grape leaves. The green borders of plates, bowls and vases give the whole piece a very satisfactory finish and strengthen the overall effect. Avoiding precious-metal preparations generally lets this decoration appear very homogeneous. The exact layout of all the trim elements can be copied from other objects and patterns, even if those may be done in gold. Original Meissen pieces, catalogs or photos are ideal for this.

For the sake of completeness, I would like to speak briefly of the modern version of grapevine decoration. It has not yet been in the Meissen catalog for long, but has provided a real enrichment of the underglaze motifs. This grapevine painting has renounced its strict discipline in favor of a looser arrangement. As a result, it also goes better with modern porcelain shapes. In addition, it shows the fruits of the grapevine, but they are painted very softly, with a gentle touch. The contours of the leaves are kept flowingly round, and the veins flow in a smooth S-curve. In terms of color, the rich green tones have been kept. Only the grapes offer a difference, since they are painted in the lightest green, and shimmer in a light gray under or even above the glaze.

The soft overall impression and the relaxed composition mean that we freely creative porcelain painters do not need a stencil. It would be a shame somehow if we would press these loose brush strokes into rank and file with a constantly repeating rhythm. One can even do without arranging the individual segments in a row on the porcelain pieces, and instead—similarly to flower painting—locate small grape arrangements (see #85, 86). These motifs also have a good effect on porcelain decorations that give the interior of a kitchen a very ornamental effect or even brighten up wine taverns suitably.

I hope that I have awakened new interest in painting experiments that you had not undertaken previously, whether out of fear of failure or from the feeling that one should devote oneself to only *one* style of painting. I am rather of the opinion that porcelain decoration offers so many techniques and decoration variations that every painter should make an effort to learn as much about them as possible and try using them when possible. Only so can one find out what one is really capable of and what comes naturally—and what does not. Only the attempt tells for sure whether fruit painting is really as difficult as it looks, or whether it offers the painter unhoped-for pleasure and makes him want to stick with this special subject. As a teacher of painting courses, I have often encountered students who noticed only when painting the individual motifs how natural this new subject was for them. For that reason, it will also be the main purpose of the new writing I plan to do in the next half-year to devote each small new volume very specially to one decoration theme.

Completed Porcelain Painting

87. A tea canister with grapevine decor. The lid of the tea canister gets just a little staffage in green on the knob, plus a border.

88. A small grapevine ensemble of Meissen porcelain, consisting of a covered pitcher, tea canister, cup, saucer and sugar bowl. It can be seen that a single piece with this decoration can also look very charming.

89. A fruit bowl with a perforated plaited foot, with grapevine decor.

90. A complete view of the large platter shown on page 77.

91. The whimsical baroque shape of this candlestick left no room for the onion pattern in its entirety. Thus it was trimmed with line staffage and scattered designs in onion-pattern blue, making it match the table service nicely.

92. The long middle section of the foot of this chalice was decorated with a couple dark rings of paint, since a fully undecorated white piece would have been unharmonious.

93. Various pieces of an onion-pattern coffee service.

94. A sugar bowl in the onion pattern.

95. The coffeepot of the same service.

96. Indian basic decoration on a plate of the "Neuer Ausschnitt" service made in Meissen.

97. Two Meissen tea canisters with Indian painting. At right is the purple Indian, which can also be had in green in the same pattern, and at left the three-leaf pattern, somewhat easier to produce. In both decorations, the border was placed on the lid of the canister.

98. A purple Indian-pattern cup, saucer and plate.

99. Indian green on a simple vase shape. The decoration is very elongated here, limited by the form, and thus appears light.[p. 96]

100. Wild fruits (blackberries, wild strawberries and wild grapes) combined with garden fruit (a cut or bitten peach). The "white flower" in the foreground, which makes the painted grapes recede into the background, has a well-conceived optical effect.

101. A plate with border of leaves and flowers.

102. A medium-sized wall plate with a rich mushroom still-life. We can see clearly that the main motif is "anchored" centrally in a clump of grass—unlike flower bouquets that "float" on the white porcelain.

103, 104. Closely related to hunting painting is bird painting. Both techniques are painted wet on wet and can be varied as one wishes by replacing details (branches, landscape). While the kingfisher appears with his catch in the example at right, the little robin brightens up the cup and plate of the coffee service on the left.

105. The toucan is presumably at home in exotic jungles.

106. A Meissen cake plate with laterally displaced bouquet painting, circa 1800.

107. Painting on a Meissen coffee cover in the form of the "Grosser Ausschnitt", by Uwe Geissler, 1983.

108. In comparison, the more graphic technique of the Berlin factory on a tray.

109. Probably Meissen's best-known porcelain shape, the "Neuer Ausschnitt" with finely painted small roses, one of the many subgroups of manneristic painting.

110. Flower painting on a saucer, with very nice threefold division of the central motif into main flower, binding flower and crossing.

111. A very loosely painted rose bouquet in the center of a dessert platter sprayed cobalt blue.

112. A well-painted Alpine violet on a vase.

113. The flowers on these old Berlin cups of the KPM have served the scholars of porcelain painting as models for many years.

114, 115. The two show sides of a so-called snake-handle vase, additionally decorated with gold staffage.

116, 117. Two examples of rose painting, the one below painted in the classic manner.

119. Not only scattered flowers, but small animals also appear livelier on an uneven surface, just as if they were alive.

118. An original decoration design by the author. The three-dimensional nature of the plate, and the piercings in the flange in particular, let the gracefully painted flowers look as if one were seeing them through a cutout in the plate.

120. Meissen bouquets run around a sugar bowl.

122. This cup is decorated not only with flower bouquets, but also with a swan's-neck handle.

122. This cup is decorated not only with flower bouquets, but also with a swan's-neck handle.

123. A bowl and a candlestick, matching the service shown above.

124. These cherries look good enough to eat! The edge of the round fruit bowl is decorated in gold staffage.

A Short History of the Development of Meissen Painting

Since the development of the first European hard porcelain by Johann Friedrich Böttger and Walther von Tschirnaus in 1708-09, incessant experimentation with decoration and paint production has, of course, gone on. The Far Eastern patterns could not be taken over without modification, and the recipes were then real secrets of high material value.

The name of Johann Gregor Höroldt is surely known to every Meissen fan, and it is really impressive to see what a wealth of color we owe to him. As early as 1731, just 21 years after the founding of the Meissen factory, a palette of sixteen on-glaze colors was available for use there. This was an enormous achievement for Höroldt, especially when one thinks of how much time the Chinese alchemists had at their disposal. He was able to do it only by carrying out a long series of experiments with countless tests and mixing experiments. And he was able to include the experiences of David Köhler, who shared his secret with him just before his death on April 30, 1723—at that time quite a normal procedure, since so many alchemists spent their lives paying strict attention to keeping any spies away from them. Any recipes and mixtures that were found guaranteed great recognition at court. It was also Köhler who made significant improvements to the well-known underglaze painting.

In the 18th century, paints were rather hard in appearance and dull in sheen. This explains the very brittle appearance of the so-called "copperplate painting" that, because of this appearance, is still called "dry flower painting" today. Copperplate engravings were the most often-used form of porcelain patterns at that time: nature studies, illustrations of the trends of the times, landscapes were made in this manner just as were portraits, maps or animal pictures. It is really astonishing how precisely stripe on stripe was delineated in this special painting technique, thus creating a very fine-lined motif. The almost microscopically precise reproduction of nature invites one on a voyage of discovery through the entire picture: every hair on the leg of an insect and the fine points of thin grasses are detailed. Even today—after all the changes in Meissen painting—copperplate decorations enjoy great popularity and are also a welcome addition to the hobby painter's learning program.

This technique, of course, portrays things completely unprotected, naturalistically correct, which means that even wrinkled leaves, crooked stems, dull colors and chewed-up fruits are shown, which today repels many an observer who wants colorful decorations on his table service to radiate freshness and look appetizing. This kind of taste, though, was developed only much later, long after Höroldt. This was, of course, brought on by the constant development of paints and painting techniques as well as the burning process.

When one reflects that in the beginning the goods to be burned were pushed into the preheated muffle on a sheet of metal, so they could be pulled out again when they had attained a certain glow of color, one can probably see that a good burning depended about 30% on luck. A great achievement of its time was the development of the underglaze blue, which was already available in its best quality in 1735 and was used from 1739 on for the completed version of the onion pattern. The Meissen paint recipes did not, though, remain a well-kept secret for long in the years that followed, since painters soon became journeymen and spread the secrets through all of Europe.

The painting shows a great deal of fast development in execution and color. And the Marcolini era (1774-1815) was still to come, with many kinds of loose flower painting which, to be sure, also drew a lot of criticism. Described as "commercial painting", it was used to cover faults in the porcelain and attract mass sales. The variety of decorations and the typical "Marcolini tulips", which look especially elegant with their black features in the blossoms and are still charming to look at today, are interesting characteristics of this era—though today they are, unfortunately, painted only rarely.

Along with the flower painting, though, there also arose the Indian decorations taken from the Far Eastern "Chinoiserie": red court dragons, yellow lions or flying dogs are to this day the characteristics of perfect decoration with a high degree of ornamental liveliness and classic restraint, creating a unified impression.

Even these decorations can appear rather dull on old pieces produced in Meissen, as well as seemingly flowing. The constantly developing progress in painting materials and burning technology had also made the patterns of Indian painting more perfect and their overall impression more beautiful. Only the present form of the drawing pen would have been worth a great deal to the masters of those times.

At that time it was important to find a suitable means of bringing formal decoration (Staffage) and painting into harmony. Often the painted surface decoration fell short of the opulent shapes of the individual porcelain pieces, and efforts were made to find a balanced blend. Naturally, one should not forget that Hörold's excellent paintings awakened the jealousy of the other great Meissen master, Johann Joachim Kaendler. His three-dimensional porcelain works are unequaled to this day. He treasured the elegance of the natural in shaping and put this into practice as well. When one looks at his creations, one sees details of feet, handles, knobs and the like carried through to the finest bit. The painters wanted to achieve the same thing, and practiced it in the then incomparable style of Antoine Watteau. This painting, done in copper green, was able to assert itself very well against the lively three-dimensional forms that surrounded it. But in other motifs as well, more naturalness was soon required, and the paintings based on so many Chinese originals were even regarded as primitive. The trend went all the more toward the three-dimensional and away from flat stylized animals, buildings and figures.

Those who ordered these products also wanted more and more to see botanically correct flowers, and so it was decided to bring painters from "outside" into the factory to give training to the "painter corps". One of them was the Dresden painter Heinrich Jakob Fehling, who brought his assistant Augustin Hoffmann. The resulting naturalistic portrayal of the most varied motifs on porcelain now grew progressively more out of harmony with the porcelain itself. A painful dissonance was spoken of when what was almost a natural science encyclopedia was applied with expert strokes to the whimsical rococo shapes of relief-patterned porcelain. Only the strictly classic shapes of later days offered sufficient smooth surfaces for a clear dominance of the painted picture.

In the process, porcelain became a painting surface like linen, wood, paper and the like. In the Marcolini era, the color palette had advanced so much that even the paintings of renowned masters, which had nothing to do with the decoration of porcelain, were copied on the "white gold". A painter who could reproduce these decorations, which were usually technically difficult to create, was rightfully regarded as more than usually talented. Even today this genre of decoration is the one that demands the greatest wealth of experience in the use of porcelain paints. Around 1770, Johann Georg Loehning was one of these few masters to whom we are indebted for a variety of enchanting miniature portraits. On small, simple plates, without fluting and thus forming an ideal background for painting, he created what was probably the very essence of realistic portrait art in Meissen.

In the early nineteenth century, the work of one of Germany's most significant artists, Ludwig

Richter, is worthy of note. Unfortunately, his influence on porcelain art was not very great, since the "closed minds" of the people at Meissen hindered him greatly and he regarded the cramped atmosphere of the painting rooms as a limitation on his creativity—he even had to fight for permission to take his painting students on a field trip into the beautiful Elbe Valley!

In the times that followed, more and more trends toward industrialization appeared at the factory, which threatened to have catastrophic effects on the artistic worth of the painting. Under Heinrich Gottlieb Kühn, commercial success seemed to be more important than the high artistic quality of the painting. Colors were subordinated to gold, and pomposity was expressed by the pieces of porcelain. The introduction of gloss gold, which eliminated the laborious job of polishing, allowed the same production in less time. At that time too, the porcelain manufacturers flirted with the still-new developments known as copper printing and lithography. Kühn was trying hard to turn the premises into a real factory. Even though sales figures justified him, the artistic niveau of Meissen porcelain hit a low level that can be traced into the twentieth century.

But even in those times there was no shortage of outstanding artists who tried to save the reputation of the Meissen factory. We can mention the later artistic director Franz Andreas Weger, who became famous for his expressive portrait plaques; then the adoption of the paste-to-paste painting, developed in Sèvres, by the Meissen painters. The absolute high point in development, though, was embodied in a man whose imaginative flower paintings in the style of the "Founding Years" of the seventies can still make any artist in any factory turn pale today: Julius Eduard Braunsdorf. Created with the supreme self-assurance of a sleepwalker, these flower arrangements, usually on large plates, captured the aroma and glorious colors of nature so convincingly that they enchanted the beholder like practically no other artistic style. He knew better than any other how to match the composition to the existing object.

He also possessed true mastery in his exact knowledge of the burning reactions, that is, how the paints changed their tones during burning. I believe it is this situation that makes porcelain painting a difficult art. Nothing is finished after the last brush stroke. All the nuances of color can change in the burning and influence a work for good or ill. Being able to foresee this and mix the colors deliberately is the true skill that one gains only after many years and hundreds of painted pieces. Painters with a routine established over decades can even mix glowing rose tints in such a way that out of them, in the fire, a desired warm, gray shadow tone, that looks like the result of chance to the layman, is created. This unbelievable mastery of color was shown by Braunsdorf in countless exemplary, brilliant creations.

Along with all this, there was naturally mass production, with pieces being produced in constantly repeating series in the manneristic painting style that had meanwhile become customary. Flowers, fruits and other motifs gradually took on an appearance typical of them. The monotony of mass production naturally brings the frequent result that the flowers look uniformly boring and lose all freshness and elegance that one wants in these natural pictures. This can be seen often in the "Purple Rose" decoration.

In manneristic painting, though, there were and still are the refreshing identifying marks of artists who, in the situation where they had to prepare a piece in a certain length of time, did the work in such a way that they created the best possible effect with the fewest strokes. In the period around 1920, this quick, colorful painting style reached its zenith. When one looks at these pieces today, one is excited to see how freely the work was done. On bright flower leaves, one does not see striped-in shadowed areas, but clear, dark shadows that could be painted very quickly and yet have a good effect.

Naturally, we must not forget the paintings that Art Nouveau brought onto Meissen porcelain. Although at this time there was more creative work done in the realm of three-dimensional figures, several interesting services with decorations that were very atypical of Meissen also attract attention. The new feeling for form was also reflected in new service designs, which demanded differently constituted decoration variations. A break was to be made with the historical models, and tempestuous progress was to be proclaimed. Thus even an architect was hired to design a tea service. Henry van de Velde created this design, to be sure, but was not able to have any lasting effect on the "catapult decor" of the Meissen chinaware style. As so often, someone came in and wanted to bring new ideas from outside. Anything that did not develop out of the old tradition never had any apparent chance of succeeding in Meissen.

And so typical Meissen flowers are painted to this day, even though in this century there have been many attempts made to try something new. We need only think of the wall-picture designs, that undoubtedly achieved their zenith with the "Fürstenzug" (100 x 10 meters). On the other hands, the attempts made in the fifties and sixties, that caused even tolerant observers to shake their heads, were terrible, even though wall plates and the like have been a popular playground for painters for ages, where they could paint motifs that simply did not belong on table services. Paintings on porcelain with a richly worked frame are ranked today among the greatest art treasures in the museums. For the hobby painter it also helps that plates of porcelain are very easy to handle and, in their variety, allow any desired shape. In the most recent years, even the renowned onion design has been offered by Meissen on wall plates.

With all the painting styles used on Meissen porcelain over the centuries, a tremendous variety of variation has come into being and allowed us to create decorations of many kinds. Thank God, we no longer have any problems with color recipes, burning secrets or bad-quality porcelain. For you in the hobby realm, the Meissen decoration archives, that can be found scattered all over the world, offer good opportunities to reproduce these paintings in your own efforts.

Appendix

AGATE ROD: A semi-precious stone of the finest structure, with which one can bring matte gold to an elegant high gloss.

AIRBRUSH TECHNIQUE : Application of tempera, acrylic, porcelain or other paints with a jet of air (pressure about 2.5 bar).

ALLSTABILO PENCIL: A special grease pencil (such as No. 8008) that can be used to lay out designs, the lines of which will burn off during burning.

BISCUIT PORCELAIN: Unglazed, burned porcelain, which can also be achieved by "popping off the glaze".

BONE CHINA: English bone porcelain, in which the calcium phosphate of burned cattle bones serves as the flux.

CERAMIC MASS: Massive porcelain in liquid form, particularly suitable for casting, such as of figures.

CHINESE STYLE : Designs taken from Chinese art and culture, often disrupted with added European features.

COPPER ENAMEL: Powdered enamel in transparent or opaque form, which adheres only to biscuit porcelain.

COVERING PAINT: A somewhat fluid mass that, after application, hardens into a stiff foil and can be removed without difficulty.

CRAQUELÉ: Fine hairline cracks in ceramic glazes, resulting from uneven hardening of glaze layers, or of the porcelain and the glaze layer.

DECORATING: Ornamenting the white porcelain in one or more colors. Hand-painted or stamped decorations of many kinds can be made. Colorful or golden borders and various glazing techniques are also involved.

DETAILING: Augmenting the basic painting with all sorts of fine details, such as shadowing, washing or marking.

ERASER: A tool with which burned-in gold and luster can be removed.

FLAKING: Reaction of paint when put on too heavily. Bubbles or cracks result after burning.

FLANGE: The outer rim of a plate, from the lower central area to the edge.

FLUX: A substance that lowers the melting point of a paint, mass or glaze material (minium, lead carbonate).

FOND: An evenly applied one-color surface which may include unpainted white areas.

GOLDEN CUT: Harmonious dividing principle of a line or surface, in which the smaller area relates to the larger as it relates to the whole (3:5, 5:8, 8:13, etc.).

GRID: A tool with cross-hatched lines, used to maintain correct proportions when transferring designs of complex motifs.

INDIA INK: East Indian ink that burns away in burning.

KOPAIVA BALSAM: A painting material made of the resin of a tropical tree.

LAYOUT: Second work process after drawing the design (Aufzeichnen), in which the essential elements of the motif are painted on.

LUSTER: Metallic salts that give the porcelain an iridescent high gloss.

MANNERISM: Painting in the style of copperplate painting for often-repeated decorations, such as in Meissen flower painting.

MEDIUM: Substance used to adapt the powdered paint, such as turpentine, oil of cloves, thickened balsam (resinous turpentine).

MIXING OIL: Non-drying oil for mixing paint (made of 13 parts oil of cloves, 26 parts lavender oil and 200 parts mineral oil).

MUFFLE OVEN: An electric burning oven with thick insulation. On its upper surface there is usually a vapor chimney, and in the door a window. The heating coils usually run along the inner walls.

OIL PREPARATION: Slow thickening of turpentine into thick oil in up to three nested containers.

OXIDE PAINT: Porcelain paint made of metallic oxides and able to melt well in burning with the right addition of flux.

PEN DRAWING: Drawing done with the steel pen.

PIECE: General term for any kind of porcelain object.

PRECIOUS METALS: Gold, silver and platinum paint, with the subcategories of gloss, polished and matte gold, silver and platinum.

SCATTERINGS: Small decoration elements (flowers, insects, fruits, etc.) as added decoration around the main motif or to conceal flaws in the porcelain or glaze unobtrusively.

SEGERKEGEL: A pyramid-shaped ceramic device to determine oven temperatures.

SQUIRREL HAIR: The finest brush hair, made from the tail hairs of a Siberian squirrel.

STAFFAGE: Decoration of three-dimensional elements on dishes and figures.

STENCIL: A means of quick drawing of a pattern, usually made of metal foil in which the outlines of the design are cut. Charcoal is applied to the porcelain through these cuts. Especially handy for beginners or for preparing large quantities with the same design (Indian painting).

STRUCTURE POWDER: Non-transparent melting paint with which reliefs and structures can be applied.

SURFACE DECORATION: A painting or stamping that takes in the entire white surface of a porcelain object and thus leaves hardly any white areas (especially suitable for flawed porcelain).

WORKTABLE: A raised working surface to support the painter's brush arm. The U-shaped cutout allows optimal holding of the piece to be painted.

Bibliography

Demel, Erich. *Porzellanmalerei*. Zürich: 1979.

Enlin, Yang. *Chinesische Porzellanmalerei*. Leipzig: 1986.

Friedel, Peter. *Porzellan und Keramik bemalen—mein Hobby,* Munich 1982.

Hillebrecht, Bente, & Janet Schnidt. *Porzellanmalerei*. Stuttgart: 1987.

Imhof, Phyllis. *Aparte Porzellanmalerei*. Freiburg: 1985.

Jaennicke, Friedrich. *Handbuch der Porzellan-, Steingut- und Fayance-Malerei*. Stuttgart: 1987 (reprint of 1891 edition).

Just, Johannes. *Meissener Jugendstilporzellan*. Leipzig: 1983.

Kesten, Brigitte. *Charakteristik der Porzellanfarben*. Stuttgart: 1984.

Koustrup, Birthe. *Verschiedene Bücher für Porzellanmalen*. Holte (DK): 1984.

Kretzschmar-Volck, Hedwig. *Fliesenmalerei*. Bonn: 1981.

———. *Porzellanmalerei*. Bonn: 1981.

Lumm, Rudolf. *Porzellanmalerei*. Stuttgart, 1984.

Lupfer, E. A. *Ornate Pictorial Calligraphy*. New York: 1982.

Mields, Martin. *Praxis der Porzellanmalerei*. Munich: 1965.

Muehe, Iris. *Porzellanmalerei. Eine alte japanische Technik*. Stuttgart: 1990.

Polla, Ursula. *Porzellanmalerei. Eine Anleitung zu verschiedenen Techniken*. Stuttgart: 1990.

Porzellan-Lexikon. Munich: 1979.

Rudolph, Wolfgang. *Seemansandenken*. Leipzig: 1985.

Viggiani, Dantella. *Die Kunst der Porzellanmalerei*. Stuttgart: 1985.

Photo Credits

The photographs, unless otherwise noted, were provided by the author.

The slides for the building painting (Meissen Cathedral) and the black-and-white photographs of the onion pattern were taken by the Fotostudio Aurel Beer in Rösrath.

The color slides of the porcelain paintings were taken by the Fotostudio Unger in Cologne.

Illustrations 57 and 58 are published here with the kind permission of the Popp-Verlag of Heidelberg.

Translator's Note

I am indebted to my wife Pat and her copy of *Taylor's Encyclopedia of Gardening* for the correct English names of the painted flowers. If only I could say the same about mushrooms!

Uwe Geissler

The author, Uwe Geissler, was active at the State Manufactory in Meissen from 1973 to 1984. He is capable of sharing with the layman the particular charm of true Meissen painting through his drawings and photos. He maintains his porcelain studio at Lintgasse 10, Cologne, not far from the Old Market, and teaches porcelain painting. For information and advice on problems, he can be reached at D-51503 Rösrath, Hauptstrasse 76, telephone and fax number 02205/3108.